Where in the World Can I . . .

TALK TO ANIMALS?

Where in the World Can I . . .
TALK TO
ANIMALS?
WORLD
BOOK
www.worldbook.com

World Book, Inc.
180 North LaSalle Street, Suite 900
Chicago, Illinois 60601
USA

For information about other World Book publications, visit our website at **www.worldbook.com** or call **1-800-WORLDBK (967-5325).**

For information about sales to schools and libraries, call 1-800-975-3250 (United States), or 1-800-837-5365 (Canada).

© 2023 (print and e-book) by World Book, Inc. All rights reserved. No part of this publication may be reproduced, stored in a retrieval system, or transmitted in any form or by any means (electronic, mechanical, photocopying, recording, or otherwise) without written permission from World Book, Inc.

WORLD BOOK and the GLOBE DEVICE are registered trademarks or trademarks of World Book, Inc.

Library of Congress Cataloging-in-Publication Data for this volume has been applied for.

Where in the World Can I…
ISBN: 978-0-7166-5251-9 (set, hc.)

Talk to Animals?
ISBN: 978-0-7166-5255-7 (hc.)
ISBN: 978-0-7166-5267-0 (pf.)

Also available as:
ISBN: 978-0-7166-5261-8 (e-book)

STAFF

Executive Committee
President
Geoff Broderick

Vice President, Editorial
Tom Evans

Vice President, Finance
Donald D. Keller

Vice President, International
Eddy Kisman

Vice President, Technology
Jason Dole

Director, Human Resources
Bev Ecker

Editorial
Senior Editor
Shawn Brennan

Curriculum Designer
Caroline Davidson

Proofreader
Nathalie Strassheim

Graphics and Design
Senior Visual Communications Designer
Melanie Bender

Coordinator, Design Development and Production
Brenda Tropinski

Senior Media Editor
Rosalia Bledsoe

Acknowledgments
Writer: Cynthia O'Brien

Produced by
Focus Strategic Communications Inc.

TABLE OF CONTENTS

TALKING TO ANIMALS

People *communicate* (give and receive information) in many different ways. We use language when we speak or write words. There are thousands of languages spoken around the world.

People also use facial expressions, such as smiling, to communicate feelings like happiness. A gesture, such as a nod, is another way of saying "yes."

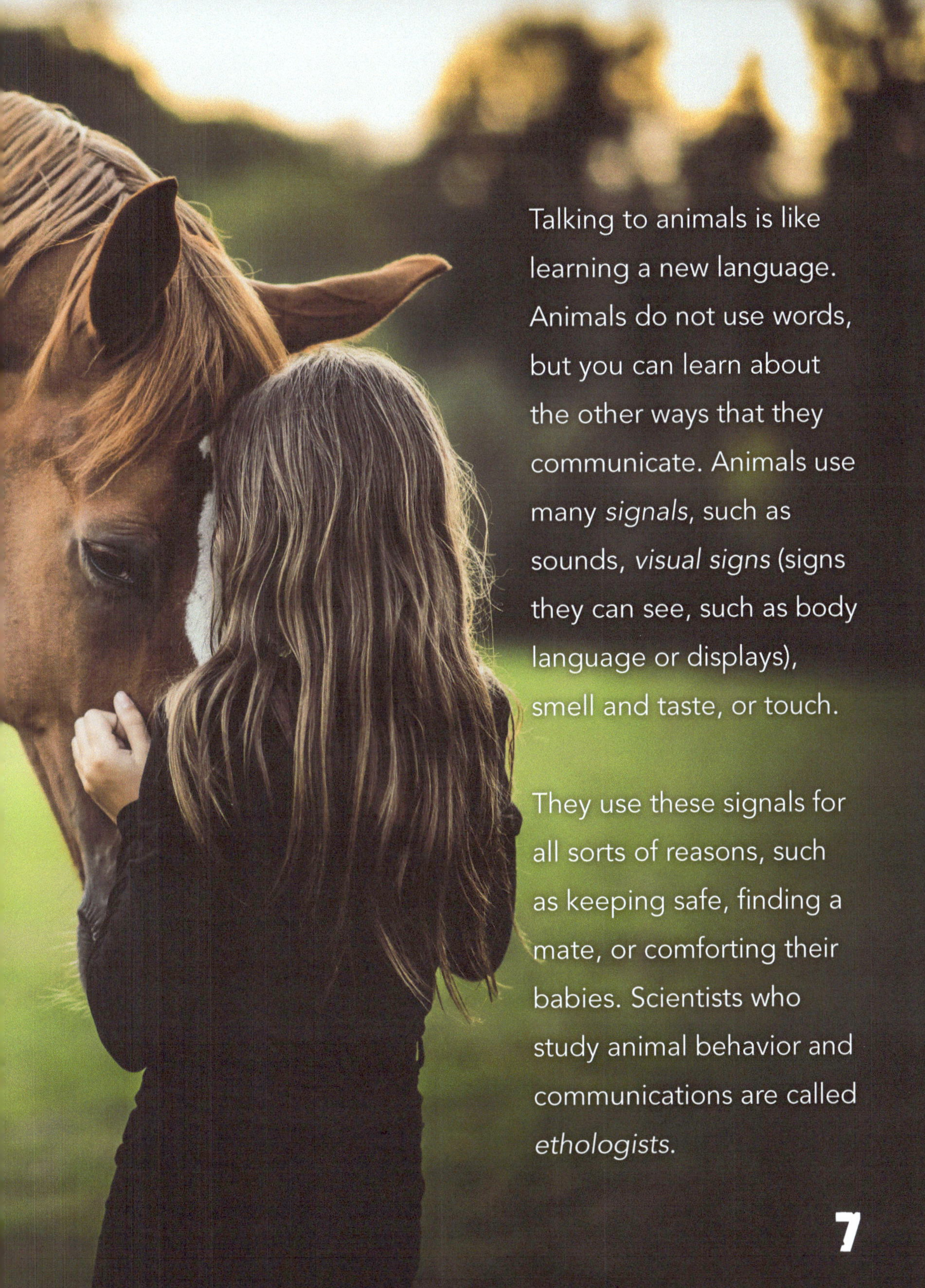

Talking to animals is like learning a new language. Animals do not use words, but you can learn about the other ways that they communicate. Animals use many *signals*, such as sounds, *visual signs* (signs they can see, such as body language or displays), smell and taste, or touch.

They use these signals for all sorts of reasons, such as keeping safe, finding a mate, or comforting their babies. Scientists who study animal behavior and communications are called *ethologists*.

You may know a lot of animal sounds, such as a cow's moo or a lion's roar. But did you know that a loud moo may mean a cow is looking for her calf? A low, quiet moo means the cow is talking to her calf. Lions roar to protect their territory, but they make a low gurgling noise when they are happy.

Many animals attract a mate using sound. Bullfrogs croak to attract a mate. Some birds sing.

Male red deer make deep calls to appear bigger and stronger to a female deer. Male humpback whales sing for hours when trying to attract females, but also when communicating with other whales far away.

Other animal sounds are like alarms. Vervet monkeys make different warning sounds for different *predators* (animals that hunt other animals for food) they spot. For example, when a leopard is present, the monkeys' call will warn others in the group to go high in the trees. An eagle warning call indicates the need for the group to find safety on the ground.

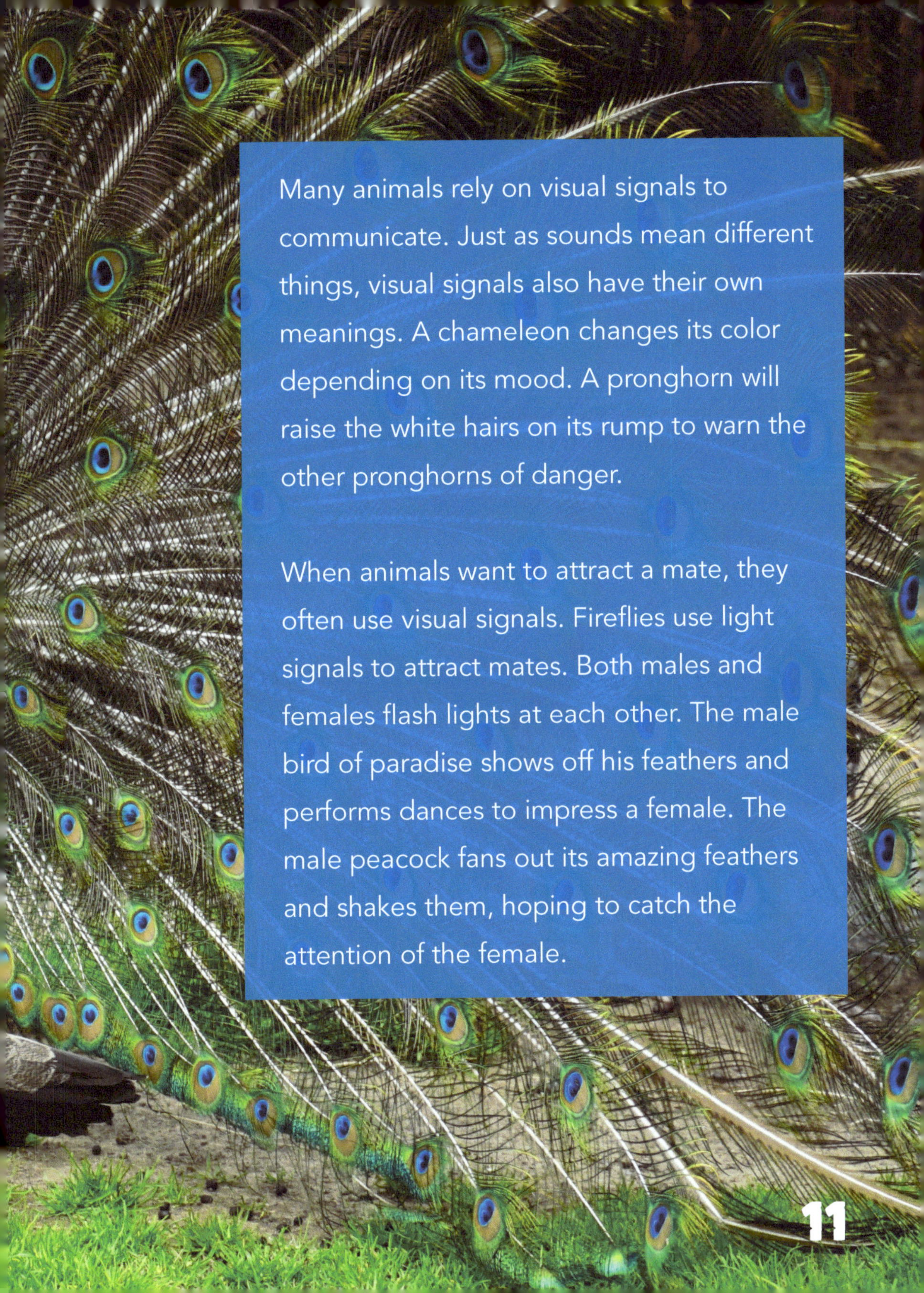

Many animals rely on visual signals to communicate. Just as sounds mean different things, visual signals also have their own meanings. A chameleon changes its color depending on its mood. A pronghorn will raise the white hairs on its rump to warn the other pronghorns of danger.

When animals want to attract a mate, they often use visual signals. Fireflies use light signals to attract mates. Both males and females flash lights at each other. The male bird of paradise shows off his feathers and performs dances to impress a female. The male peacock fans out its amazing feathers and shakes them, hoping to catch the attention of the female.

Smell and touch are also powerful senses that animals use. Insects, mammals, and many fish produce chemicals called *pheromones (FAIR uh moans).* Other animals pick up the scent of these chemicals. For example, a mountain lion will urinate to mark its territory. This warns others to stay away. Such animals as deer recognize their family members by smell. Snakes stick their tongues out to detect the pheromones of their prey.

Animals use touch to comfort or bond with each other or to show who's boss. Horses touch noses to say hello. Mothers of many species often touch their young. Just as you wash to keep clean, animals *groom*. To communicate affection or family ties, many animals *groom* each other. The animals clean each other to get rid of things, such as leaves, dirt, or bugs.

Some animals are better at understanding people than others. Gorillas, elephants, and dolphins are all amazing communicators. These animals have become famous for their skills. Koko was a western lowland gorilla that learned to understand 2,000 words of spoken English and more than 1,000 signs of American Sign Language (ASL). Koko, who was born in the San Francisco Zoo, started learning ASL when she was just one year old.

Other animals have learned human words, too. Dogs know many commands, such as sit, but they may understand even more words. Chaser was a border collie that lived with Dr. John Pilley in South Carolina in the United States. Dr. Pilley began teaching Chaser words when she was a two-month old puppy. Chaser learned more than 1,000 words.

African grey parrots are clever birds. The most famous was Alex, who knew over 100 words. He could also recognize over 50 objects and count up to six.

If you have a pet, you probably talk to animals already. How do you let your dog know that it is time for a walk? Does your cat meow when it is time for dinner? Animals also show us when they are happy, sad, or in need of our attention.

New technology might make it even easier for people to communicate with animals. For example, scientists are working on computerized systems that dogs can use to interact with us. There are other studies being done on prairie dogs, dolphins, and other animals that may help animals and people understand each other better in the future.

Over the next pages, discover where you can talk to elephants, dolphins, and other animals.

PHUKET ELEPHANT SANCTUARY

Sanctuaries rescue and protect elephants. This is important because, for many years, people have hunted African elephants for their tusks and used Asian elephants for work or entertainment. Also, many elephants have lost their *habitat* (where they usually live). Elephants are now *endangered* animals. These are animals that are at risk of dying out.

The Phuket Elephant Sanctuary gives Asian elephants a chance to roam freely. It is a 30-acre (12-hectare) park in Pa Klok, northeastern Phuket, Thailand. When you visit the sanctuary, you learn about elephants in a natural setting and have a chance to meet them. As you spend time at the Phuket sanctuary, watch and listen to the elephants to see if you can tell what they are saying.

Elephants are very intelligent animals and great communicators. They live in groups called *herds*. An older female elephant leads the herd. Elephants make many sounds, including different rumbling sounds, snorts, and grunts. When they say hello, elephants make low rumbling sounds, shake their ears, and touch trunks. The leader of the herd flaps her ears and makes a different rumbling sound when she wants the others to follow her. Elephants recognize the voices of their herd members, even from very far away. They also "hear" with their feet by picking up vibrations in the ground.

Elephants love to play and may make trumpeting sounds when they are excited or having fun. But a loud trumpeting sound can mean an elephant is frightened. You will hear many elephant sounds when you spend a morning or afternoon at the sanctuary.

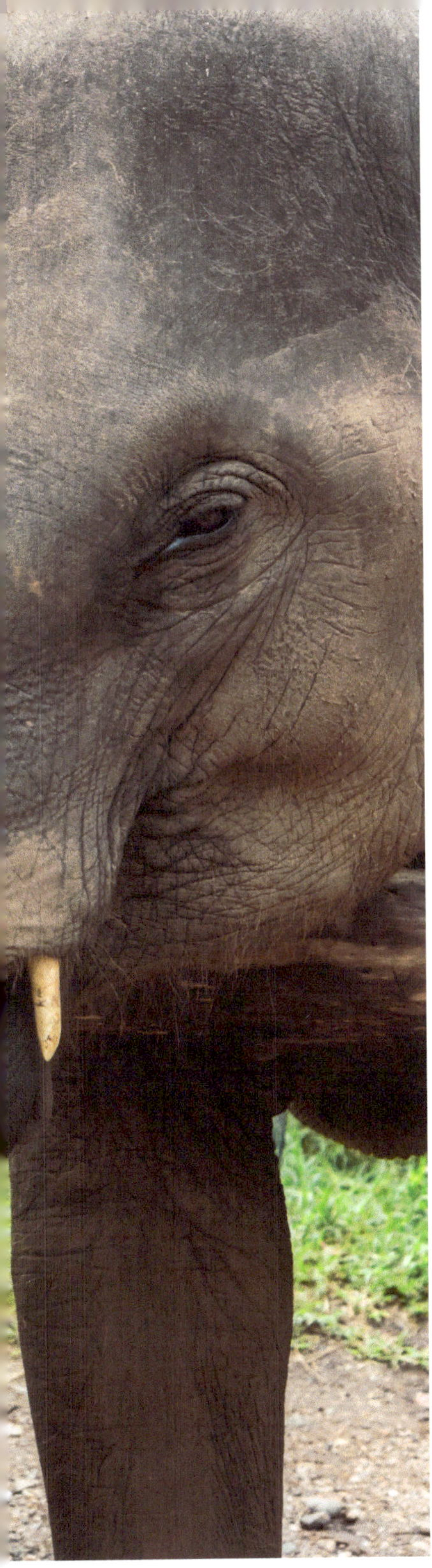

What does an elephant do all day? You can spend a whole day at the sanctuary to find out. This is an amazing way to spend some up-close time with the elephants. Starting in the morning, you will feed the animals and then watch them swim and play. During the day, the guides at the sanctuary will teach you about elephant communication and behavior. Think about what you have learned while watching the elephants. You may see an elephant put its trunk in another elephant's mouth. This is how elephants hug each other.

In the afternoon, the guide will take you to meet the elephants. Try talking to them! You will help prepare some rice balls and fruit for the elephants to eat. Elephants are *herbivores* (plant eaters). They will be very happy to see you at feeding time.

A great way to see how elephants behave is to go on the sanctuary's canopy walkway. The raised walkway is 1,969 feet (600 meters) long. The tour guide will tell you all about the elephants as you watch from high above. This is a great way to see the elephants interact with each other. After the walk, you can meet the elephants up close and help to feed them.

When you are over 18 years of age, you can volunteer at the sanctuary for one day, three days, or a week. This is an opportunity to learn from the experts at the sanctuary and spend a lot of time with the elephants. You can also visit elephants at Elephant Nature Park in Mae Taeng District, Chiang Mai, Thailand. This park is mainly a place for rescued elephants, but it protects other animals as well.

XISHUANGBANNA NATIONAL NATURE RESERVE

An amazingly rich variety of animals and plants live in China's Xishuangbanna National Nature Reserve. The reserve is divided into five areas and contains tropical rainforest and a mix of other forest types. It covers a vast area on the southwest tip of Yunnan province. Many of the animals and plants there are rare or endangered, such as the northern white-cheeked gibbon.

More than 90% of China's wild elephants live in the reserve in an area called Wild Elephant Valley. You can watch the elephants. You might spot some water buffalo, too. Altogether the reserve is home to more than 100 types of mammals, 400 species of birds, 63 species of reptiles, and 100 fish species.

There are guided tours of different parts of the reserve. In the Sky Tree Scenic Park, you can take a walk 118 feet (36 meters) above the rainforest floor.

SAN DIEGO ZOO AND SAFARI PARK

Do you want to talk to a bonobo or spend time with a polar bear? San Diego Zoo is the place to go. The zoo is home to over 12,000 animals! To get there, go to Balboa Park, just north of downtown San Diego, California. The zoo covers over 100 acres (40 hectares) of land in the park.

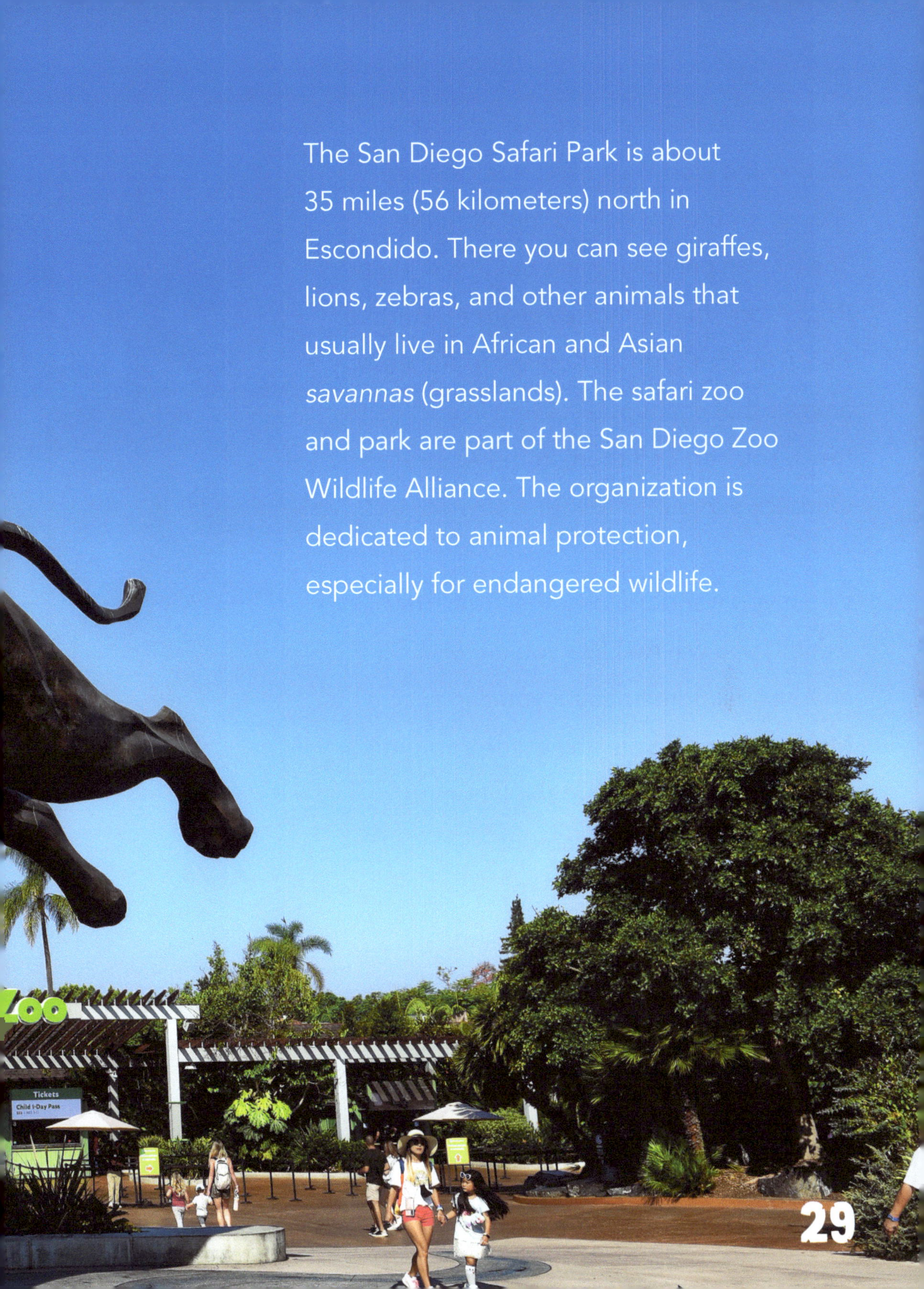

The San Diego Safari Park is about 35 miles (56 kilometers) north in Escondido. There you can see giraffes, lions, zebras, and other animals that usually live in African and Asian *savannas* (grasslands). The safari zoo and park are part of the San Diego Zoo Wildlife Alliance. The organization is dedicated to animal protection, especially for endangered wildlife.

Animals live in different kinds of habitats around the world. The zoo has created spaces for the animals to feel at home. The African penguins hang out in the Africa Rocks zone that is modeled after Boulders Beach in South Africa. Koalas are Australian animals that are happiest living in eucalyptus trees. You can find them in the Australian Outback exhibit.

When you wander along the Tiger Trail exhibit, you will feel like you are visiting an Asian rainforest. See if you can spot a Malayan tiger. If you stay at the zoo until evening, you might hear the laughing kookaburra making its famous call in one of two *aviaries* (enclosures for birds).

The Wildlife Explorers Basecamp is an area of the zoo especially for young animal lovers. It is a place to play and interact with all sorts of animals that live in different kinds of habitats. For example, you can meet a tortoise or a caiman in the Rainforest zone. While you are there, pop into the Spineless Marvels building to discover how insects and spiders interact with each other.

Prairie dogs cuddle, kiss, and make many different sounds. They have specific chirps for different animals, including humans. You can visit them in the Desert Dunes zone. Then take a walk to the Wild Woods exhibit to say hello to a spider monkey. In the Marsh Meadows habitat zone, there are fish, turtles, and dwarf crocodiles to see. Also in this section is the Cool Critters building where you can visit snakes, lizards, and more.

You can talk to all the animals at the zoo, but you should not touch them. The best way to get up close to some of the animals is to take part in the Animals in Action Experience. The snow leopard is one of the animals you may see. Wildlife experts lead the sessions and are ready to answer all your questions. There may be a chance to touch or hold an animal, too.

Take an Inside Look tour if you want to get up close to certain creatures, such as flamingos. Flamingos are birds that get their bright color from the food they eat. They like to be in large groups and even perform displays together, such as a march. They do this to attract a mate. Flamingos also make honking, growling, and babbling sounds. Flamingo parents can recognize their own chick's call, even in a big crowd.

Rhinos, zebras, and other wildlife are at home in the San Diego Safari Park. This vast space includes grassland areas, forests, and desert. You can take a tour in an open-air jeep. If you get up early you can join the Sun-Up Cheetah Safari and watch the world's fastest land animal take a morning run.

During a Behind-the-Scenes Safari, guides take you to specific areas of the park. If you choose the Walkabout Australia exhibit, you can talk to kangaroos or meet a wallaby.

Both the zoo and safari park run summer camps where you can spend a week talking to the animals.

DOLPHIN RESEARCH CENTER

Bottlenose dolphins and California sea lions are waiting to meet you at the Dolphin Research Center on Grassy Key, Florida. Grassy Key is an island in the Florida Keys southwest of Key Largo. There are many day programs and a week-long dolphin camp offered at the center. When you take part in the programs or camp, you will talk with the dolphins. If you want, you can also take a swim with them.

The dolphins and sea lions live in saltwater pools along the shoreline of the Gulf of Mexico. The center protects and studies them, and invites visitors to meet these friendly creatures. A few other animals live at the center as well. There are tortoises, a beautiful hyacinth macaw, and a green iguana.

Dolphins are very friendly animals that live in groups called *pods*. Wild dolphins hunt for food together and protect each other. They also talk a lot! When you visit the Dolphin Research Center, listen to the many sounds the dolphins make.

Dolphins whistle, squeak, chirp, and make very quick sounds called clicks. Each sound means something different and each dolphin has its own, high-pitched whistle that others can recognize. This is its signature whistle, which is useful for finding each other in a big group.

Whistles are also signals that dolphins are happy or excited. For example, they whistle when they find food. Dolphins make many click sounds in a row. This is called a *click train*. Certain click trains might mean that a dolphin wants to play. Male dolphins use a different series of clicks when they want to attract females. If a young dolphin behaves badly, its mother makes loud clicks.

While you are visiting the dolphins, watch for their visual signals. Dolphins often jump out of the water, which may be a kind of contest. Think about the other things dolphins might be saying to each other. Sometimes dolphins just want to hang out with their friends. They often touch each other and jump at the same time.

If you are 10 years or older, you can sign up for the Researcher Experience for half a day or the Ultimate Trainer Program for a full day. Each program gives you lots of time to talk to the dolphins. You will also learn a lot from the center's experts. For example, you will learn to talk to the dolphins using gestures that they understand. Dolphins are very clever and can easily learn words and sentences this way.

Dolphins love to play. The Family Dolphin Splash is a fun program for all ages. Standing in shallow water, you can play all kinds of water games. Or you can go for a Dolphin Encounter to meet dolphins up close. In this program, you can kiss a dolphin or give it a handshake! You will be in both shallow and deep water for this program. The center's trainers will tell you how to communicate with the dolphins using hand signals.

Dolphins at the center will also paint a picture for you in three of the programs—Play with the Dolphin, Meet the Dolphin, and Paint with a Dolphin. You hold the canvas while the dolphin artist creates a one-of-a-kind work, just for you.

Throughout the day, the center's staff give talks about what the dolphins are doing at the time. They point out and explain what the dolphin's behavior or noise might mean. The center also has an indoor theater for other presentations.

READING FOCUS

Text Structure is all about the way a text is organized. When we know the structure, we can focus more of our energy and attention on comprehending what we read.

This book uses a Description Text Structure. It describes a topic and its characteristics using details, adjectives, and a logical order. Description texts often use examples to show and explain the main idea or topic.

Description texts usually include a lot of interesting details. We can use a graphic organizer to help us keep track of the most important information.

Prove It!

Find at least 3 examples from the text that support the claim that this book uses a Description Text Structure.

1. This is a Bubble Diagram, a strong graphic organizer for Description texts. Visit **www.worldbook.com/resources** to download and print copies or create your own!
2. As you read and/or revisit the text, complete a Bubble Diagram for EACH section:
   - Talking to Animals
   - Phuket Elephant Sanctuary
   - Xishuangbanna National Nature Reserve
   - San Diego Zoo and Safari Park
   - Dolphin Research Center
3. For each section, write the title in the center-most bubble. Next, add important details to the bubbles attached to that central, main idea. Remember, you do not have enough bubbles for *every* detail. Think critically to determine which details to include.

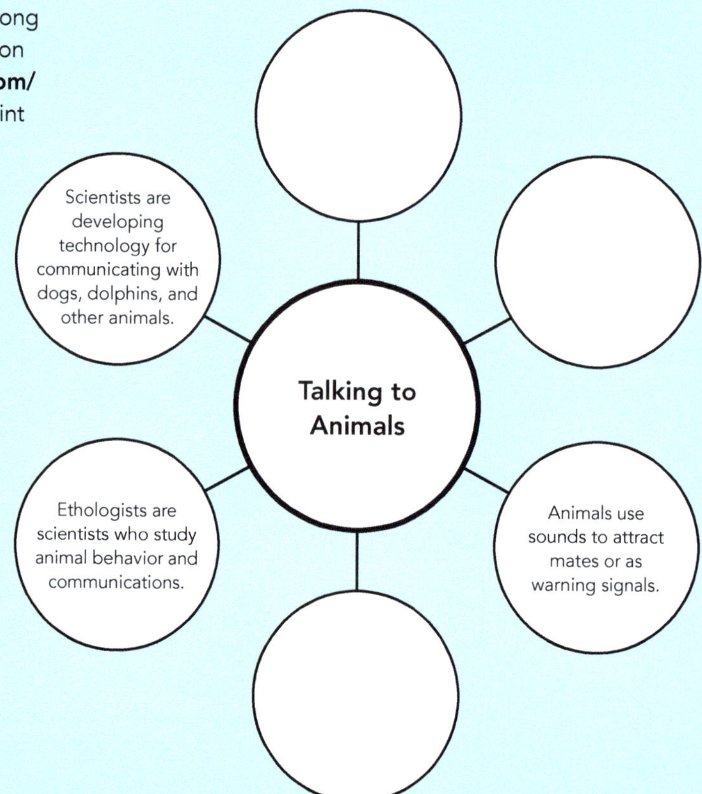

What other information about talking to animals will you add to your Bubble Diagram?

WRITING FOCUS

What do YOU think?

In your opinion, which of the four spotlighted locations would be best for talking to animals?

Review the notes you took on your Bubble Diagrams. Use evidence from the text, supported by logical reasoning, to answer the question. Your writing should include:

- A **hook** where you grab your readers' attention
- A **thesis statement** where you state your opinion
- At least 3 **reasons** why that is your opinion
- At least 3 **details** that support each reason

Use an Opinion Writing Graphic Organizer to sort through your thoughts before you write your response. Create your own or download and print a version from **www.worldbook.com/ resources.**

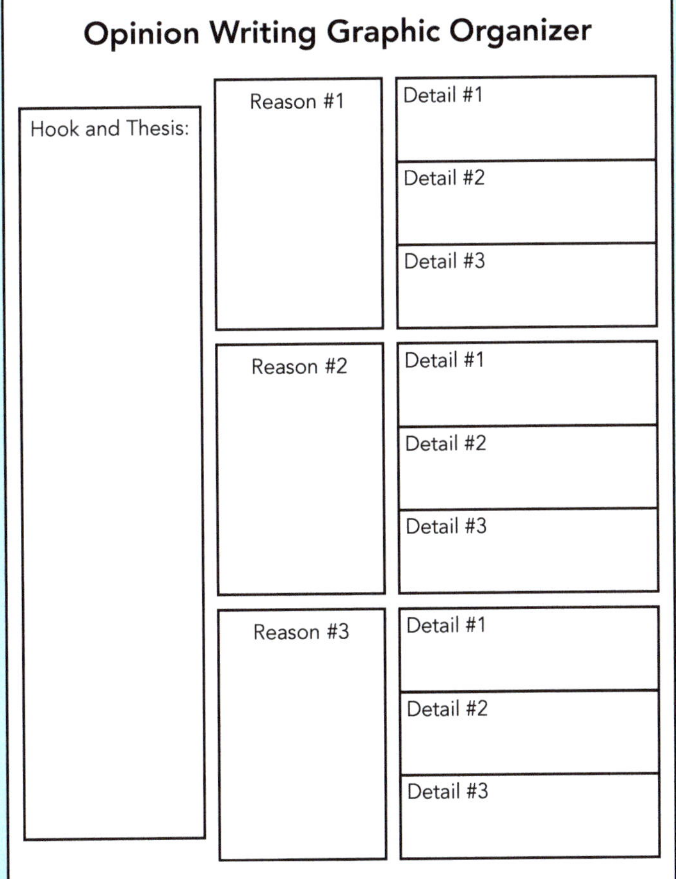

You might have noticed some words in this book written in *italics*. That means they are vocabulary terms! **Challenge yourself!** Can you include at least 5 of these words in your opinion writing?

INDEX

ACKNOWLEDGMENTS

Cover: © meunierd, Shutterstock
TP: © GoodFocused, Shutterstock
6–7 © lightpoet, Shutterstock
8–9 © Taufik Ardiansyah, Shutterstock
10–11 © Luciavonu, Shutterstock
12–13 © rbrown10, Shutterstock
14–15 © Allen.G, Shutterstock; © ZUMA Press, Alamy
16–17 © Rodica Vasiliev, Shutterstock; © Vvvita, Shutterstock
18–19 © Smokey/Stockimo, Alamy
20–21 © backpacker79, Shutterstock; © Jim O Donnell, Alamy
22–23 © Patrick Barron, Dreamstime
24–25 © SOPA Images, Alamy
26–27 © Dong Lei, Alamy; © Nagel Photography, Shutterstock
28–29 © Steven Cukrov, Dreamstime
30–31 © Smithy55, Shutterstock; © Linda Robertus, Shutterstock
32–33 © Wolfkamp, Shutterstock
34–35 © Karen Yesayan, Shutterstock
36–37 © Karen041974, Dreamstime
38–39 © Ulf Nammert, Dreamstime; © Pawel Mazur, Dreamstime
40–41 © Richard Ellis, Alamy
42–43 © Stephen Saks Photography, Alamy
44–45 © Stephen Saks Photography, Alamy

www.ingramcontent.com/pod-product-compliance
Ingram Content Group UK Ltd.
Pitfield, Milton Keynes, MK11 3LW, UK
UKHW060102300726
14090UKWH00003B/355